MW00848560

GOD ON THE MOVE

FANNING THE FLAMES OF REVIVAL

Other books by Pamela Bolton:

Ushering in Revival and Awakening

Circuit Riders—Fanning the Flames of Revival

Lady Preachers—Fanning the Flames of Revival

Today's Glory Stories—Fanning the Flames of Revival

GOD ON THE MOVE

MOVE

FANNING THE FLAMES OF REVIVAL

BY PAMELA BOLTON

Copyright © 2020 by Pamela Bolton
God on the Move
Fanning the Flames of Revival
by Pamela Bolton
Printed in the United States of America

1st Edition
ISBN: 978-0-578-63465-4

All rights reserved. The author guarantees all contents are either original or are in public domain and do not infringe upon the legal rights of any other person or work. No part of this publication may be reproduced or transmitted in any form or by any means, electronic or mechanical, including photocopying, recording, or any information storage or retrieval system, without the permission in writing from the author.

All scripture quotations are taken from the
King James Version
or the New King James Version of the Bible
Copyright © 1982 by Thomas Nelson, Inc.,
Nashville, Tennessee, United States of America

http://www.pamelabolton.com
http://outoftheboxworshipcenter.com

GOD ON THE MOVE

FANNING THE FLAMES OF REVIVAL

CONTENTS

DEDICATION

This book is also dedicated to all the "unknown" revivalists who have already gone on to Heaven as well as the many "unknown" men and women who are wholeheartedly serving God throughout the world today.

Dear Reader, I pray that this includes you.

FOREWORD

PROPHET WILLIAM EMMONS

PROPHETIC DESTINY MINISTRY, JOHNSTOWN, NY
PDMINISTRY.ORG

As I read over this book, one thing became very clear. God has and still does use the yielded lives of flawed people to release revival on the earth. They are not perfect in practice, and they don't have perfect doctrine, but what they do have is something much greater. They have a genuine passion, a spark of unrestrained love, for a perfect Saviour.

That spark of revival is present in every generation. It is stirred up by hungry Saints who are united in prayer. The breath of the Holy Spirit then blows across these surrendered souls and sets them ablaze. They may touch a single church, change a region, impact an entire nation, or send streams of His Glory around the world. However it happens, once true revival comes, no man is in control of it; and we will either embrace it and be transformed, or we will resist it and be offended.

What you hold in your hand can stir up that spark in you for more of God. May it bring to life something deep within, so you become a catalyst for His Presence and a carrier of His Glory for the next great awakening.

INTRODUCTION

God is always moving, and it's up to us to get into the flow of what He's doing today. I believe that He called me to compile this collection of old, lost revival and awakening articles that have laid buried deep in old newspapers, sometimes in libraries or attics for many years—to encourage the Church of Jesus Christ to WAKE UP to its potential today.

What is your vision for the next decade?

In God's Word, He commanded people to build memorials so that they would remember what He had done for them in the past. In a sense, this book is a memorial to what God did during a specific timeframe in our history—for His eternal purposes.

I believe that today He wants His people to dig into local, historic wells of revival in their regions in order to bring forth a fresh river of His living water in their cities, towns, and villages again. God is on the move, and He want to do even greater things than He has done in the past.

There are many well-known fathers and mothers of the faith who God used powerfully in past times of revival, and we can be encouraged by their stories. Some of them include Billy Graham, Smith Wigglesworth, William Booth, Lester Sumrall, Father Ralph DiOrio, John G. Lake, Amy Semple McPherson, Dwight L. Moody, Katherine Khulman, Charles Finney, Maria Woodworth-Etter, John Osteen, John and Charles Wesley, William Seymour, Kenneth Hagin, and Oral Roberts. Many times, the stories of mighty men and women of God are passed on by word of mouth from one generation to another, but sometimes their stories are forgotten. I'm happy that the ones included in this book were preserved in the form of newspaper articles.

My prayer is that as you read some of these accounts of revivals and about the men and women who were a part of them, that you'll be inspired to believe God for what He wants to do, right here, right now. If He did it in the past, He'll do it for us too—if we'll just trust Him. Nothing is too difficult for Him. All things are possible for those of us who believe!

I have a passion to see God move in power today, in even greater ways than He has in the past. I want to see people SAVED (Knowing who they are in Christ), DELIVERED (Completely set free), AND HEALED (Walking in complete health)! I want to be a world changer ... a powerhouse for the Kingdom of God ... a mover and a shaker; I want to see God's Kingdom come and His will be done here on Earth, as it is in Heaven. I want to be a history maker!

Do you, too? I sure hope so, because I know that you are here on this planet and called ... FOR SUCH A TIME AS THIS.

As we look back at what God has done in the past in our area, we can be encouraged to look ahead to what He wants to do right now as well as in the future. By taking a close look and building off of old foundations, we are uncapping and digging up the old wells of revival.

We can sit on the sidelines and watch others fulfill their God-given calls, or we can become active in fulfilling our own. God won't force us. We can still know Him and go to Heaven, but we can miss our call on this planet.

The choice is it up to us.... I pray that we will each choose well!

PLEASE NOTE: Any time that you see text in italics in Chapters 1-8, it is my writing. All other text in these chapters is directly quoted from newspaper articles, which are then cited at the end of each section of print. Some minor grammatical and spelling errors were corrected from the original newspapers, for clarity. When you see "???," this indicates places where the newspaper print is illegible.

CHAPTER 1

THE THIRD GREAT AWAKENING

During the late 1850s, the Third Great Awakening began in the United States, and it lasted into the early 20th century. Revival fires spread across the land, and there was scarcely a city or town that was not affected by the power of God. The following snippets are tiny snapshots of what was happening in different places across the country at that time.

Many times, throughout this book, you'll read about "union" prayer meetings. These were gatherings where all denominations met together as one in unity to pray for their cities and country, and to ask God to send revival and awakening.

RELIGIOUS REVIVALS 1858

We have alluded before to the fact that extraordinary revivals of religion are now in progress in various sections of the country. A wonderful sentiment of attention to the truths of Christianity, and a remarkable inquiry after the means of salvation, seem to pervade everywhere, and to affect all classes of community. Taking **New York** as the centre, the revival feeling has extended North through **New England and Canada**, and Westward as far as **Lake Superior**. We do not hear of it as being so prevalent or noticeable South of Virginia as elsewhere, but this is no doubt attributable to the fact that means of communication with isolated Southern communities are not abundant. Information from **Charleston, SC; Memphis, TN; and New Orleans, LA;** apprises us of an unwanted inquiry in those communities, and no doubt the diffusive feeling of religious fervor has extended through the South also, though, perhaps, not in so noticeable a degree as among the labor communities of the North. We propose to group together a few of the most prominent incidents connected with this religious awakening, that serve to show its extent and. operations.

In **Troy, NY**, there is perhaps, as little excitement as anywhere else in the State. Yet even here, a spirit of religious inquiry and fervor begins to prevail, which promises to result in large yields. Revival meetings are held at two churches—the Home Mission on Seventh Street and the Congress Street Methodist (Rev. Mr. Burdick). At the last-named church, the conversions have been numerous, and in some instances, remarkable. Several new believers have been added to the Home Mission Society. A good work is silently going on at the Third Street Baptist Church (Rev. Dr. Baldwin) at which several baptisms are to be had tomorrow morning. Special prayer meetings are held every afternoon at the rooms of the Young Men's Christian Association, in Cannon Place, which are very well attended. We hear that it is in contemplation to hold extra meetings at several churches in town which have not hitherto manifested any leading interest in the revival feeling.

In **Albany, NY**, the religious feeling has reached several churches, at which extra meetings are being held, and a large number of conversions made. Among the novelties of the season in that city, we observe that the pastors of some of the churches are engaged in the delivery of a series of lectures especially to firemen, which are very largely attended. At the church of Rev. Br. Hague, who has recently accepted a call from New York and will resign his pastorate in May, quite a feeling of interest is manifested.

In **Lansingburgh, Waterford, and Cohoes, NY,** the revival spirit has manifested itself and is working out good results. In the latter place, especially, meetings held on the evenings of weekdays attract large audiences. We do not learn that any noticeable demonstration has as yet been made in **West Troy**, though the ordinary meetings call out good audiences.

In the Methodist and Baptist churches at **Sandy Hill** (*now known as Hudson Falls, NY*), the feeling manifested is very extraordinary. Large and excited meetings are held every afternoon and evening. Conversions are very numerous. Last week, no less than twenty new believers were baptized. Clergymen from circumjacent country have been invited to take part in the meetings and many of them do so. There is no abatement in the feeling of interest since its first appearance. On the other hand, it is constantly increasing in vigor and intensity.

Revival meetings have been held every day in the Methodist and Baptist churches at **White Creek, Washington County, NY,** and attract large audiences not only of citizens, but of farmers from all the surrounding country. Two of the village churches—one Baptist and one Methodist—have **each received an addition of 100 to their membership**. The good work is still in active progress.

Hudson, NY, has been awakened and responds ardently to the furor. Extra meetings are held at every church in the city. **The Presbyterians have initiated the custom of holding meetings every afternoon at four o'clock, and the attendance upon them is quite remarkable.** Men who were seldom or never before seen at a meeting of prayer are in constant attendance there—business citizens, right from the counting-house, clerks from the counter, and artisans from the workshop in the habiliments of labor, are noticed among the auditors. The exercises consist of prayer and brief extemporaneous remarks. A placard is hung at the gate, inviting all to enter, and requesting those who cannot stay through the appointed hour to drop in for fifteen or twenty minutes. **The audience daily numbers about 500.**

In **New York City**, the feeling is general. It reaches all classes of people and is entered into most ardently by every Christian denomination. **Prayer meetings are held at schoolhouses, academies, and even in private stores.** At some of the gatherings, the most intense excitement prevails. Men have been known to run wildly through the streets, interrupting every individual with a white neckerchief they meet with the question, "What shall I do to he saved?" Prayer meetings are held every noon in the Old Middle Dutch Church, and are so largely attended by businessmen and others, that it has been found necessary to throw open three large rooms for the accommodation of the audiences. There are thirteen churches in the city at which prayer meetings are held in the daytime.

At the New School Presbyterian Church on Thirteenth Street, of which Rev. Mr. Burchard—whose lecture before our association last Winter on "The Thinker" will be remembered— is pastor, there is a great work going on. **Regular preaching has been held every night in the week except Monday and Saturday, for five weeks. The number of conversions up to the present time has been about 100. The Sunday School has recently been enlarged by the addition of nearly 100 children, gathered from the neighborhood.** On the past two Sunday afternoons, at the conclusion of the school exercises, the Superintendent requested those who desired personal conversation on the subject of religion to remain; and on each occasion, from 50 to 60 responded. A boys' prayer meeting is held once a week, and also a girls'. There are regular meetings every day at the Free Academy, which are well attended. Weekly meetings have been held there every year since 1852.

There has been from time to time much opposition and more ridicule manifested against the students towards these religious gatherings; a somewhat singular instance of which occurred a year or two ago. On one occasion shortly after the assembling of the meeting, a party of wild students, who remained in the building in consequence of a violent rain storm, with thunder and lightning, determined to employ the time in the annoyance and disturbance of the meeting. They accordingly tramped heavily up and down the halls by the door, striking it with their fists as they passed; and though they were remonstrated with, it was to no purpose. After a quarter of an hour of such injudicious sport, a vivid flash of lightning, which struck in the neighborhood, accompanied with a terrific peal of thunder, made such an impression upon the minds of three of the disturbers that they immediately desisted and knocked for entrance to the meeting. *The Tribune* says, "We understand that in connection with the stores and counting rooms of several of our most prominent merchants, private prayer meetings have been recently organized for the benefit of the clerks and other employees. They are held in some retired place in the building, secure from public intrusion, and have been of great interest and profit to those who have attended."

At the First Place Church, in **Brooklyn, NY,** a revival of extraordinary character is in progress. **There have been constant conversions for some months, and sixty persons were recently received into the church "on probation," which is the usual custom of the denomination before admitting to full "membership."** The pastor of the Church is the Rev. Cr. G. Robinson. The Sunday School has shared largely in the work, in which in addition to the above**, there have been twenty-five conversions among the elder scholars**, who have been similarly received on trial.

In Boston, MA, prayer meetings are held every morning in the Old South Church. It is stated that a family consisting of thirteen persons, have, by attending at these meetings, with one exception, been converted. **Arrangements**

have been made to begin another DAILY prayer meeting on State Street.

In **Cincinnati, OH,** the various Evangelical pastors have opened the lecture room of the First Presbyterian Church for a morning prayer meeting. It commences at 8 1/2 o'clock and continues for an hour. This is a very central location, of which the businessmen of that city avail themselves. An extraordinary interest prevails in some of the churches.

In **Philadelphia, PA,** efforts have been made to assemble the members of the Fire Department to listen to the preaching of the Gospel, and this movement has not been without decided success. **On one occasion, nearly 2,000 regular or exempt firemen attended at the National Hall in Market Street.** A deep religious interest exists in the churches, and there appears to be increased effort in the Sunday schools. The noonday prayer meetings continue with unabated interest.

Every town from **New London** to **Providence** along the coast has been subject to intense religious feeling. A powerful revival is doing its work, in which all denominations are sharing alike.

In **Hartford, CT, three lecture rooms of churches are every day filled with attendants at prayer meetings. Many conversions have taken place in the church,** including a dozen young ladies belonging to the Hartford Female Seminary.

The revival extends even to **California,** and we read of **numerous conversions in San Francisco** and **Sacramento.**

In **Utica, NY,** the revival is extending very generally to the churches. In the Corn Hill Church, **145 accessions** (*additions to the church*) **have recently been made.** At the Baptist church on Bleecker Street, **meetings are held every day at noon.**

In **Schenectady, NY,** a number of students of Union College have been converted.

In **Dubuque, IA,** several churches are experiencing revivals, and we hear of some Trojans having been converted, who, while here, however good their morals, were not noted for any particular interest in religion.

In **Cleveland, OH,** there is an extraordinary revival of religion. **A prayer meeting is held daily at 8 o'clock a. m. at the Plymouth Church, and the attendance is so large as to crowd the room.**

A Union prayer meeting is held at the Baptist Church on Pierpont Street, Brooklyn, NY, every morning at 8 o'clock, continuing for forty minutes and closing in time to allow clerks to reach New York at business hour by ferry.

Buffalo, NY, has experienced the effects of the awakening. **St. John's Church is open every morning at 9 o'clock for prayer, and we understand that not a day passes without some one of the other Churches being devoted to a similar purpose.** In short, this strange but no doubt beneficial excitement now embraces every kind of denomination except the Roman Catholic.

The Methodists, among whom revivals are a matter of frequent occurrence, have been the last to be affected by this outpouring of grace; but now that it has reached them, they enter into it with great spirit and zeal.

(The Troy Weekly Times., March 13, 1858, Page 1)

THE RELIGIOUS REVIVAL
FACTS AND INCIDENTS

There is no abatement in the great religious revival of the day. On the other hand, it is continually increasing in breadth and fervor.

All classes of religious denominations are now affected by it and have entered into the good work with the utmost spirit and fervor. **The number of conversions is entirely unprecedented. They exceed altogether those of the great awakening of half a century since.** At the West, they are numbered by thousands; a single church at **Jacksonville, IL,** numbers **1,000 new communicants.** In **New York City, that sink of wickedness and iniquity, the awakening is unprecedented. In over one hundred churches, revivals are in progress. Large numbers of people who were entirely unaccustomed to attend religious exercises are now regular attendants at the evening meetings.** Barton's Theatre has been converted into a house of worship. Daily prayer meetings are held there and are largely attended. It is on ??? that Edwin Forrest, the great tragedian, is among the recent converts.

In **Albany, NY,** the revival feeling is quite spirited. Nearly all the ministers of the evangelical churches have engaged in it.

In **Ballston Spa, Saratoga, Cohoes, and Waterford,** meetings are frequent and well attended. **Revivals are in progress in every town and village in this county.** The peculiar features of this awakening are in the highest degree interesting. They afford us some of the most striking exemplifications of character and habit, and some of the highest exhibitions of moral change. Particularly in the cases of men long given to worldly habits, who have been persuaded to abandon a course of life productive only of evil to themselves and community and adopt one measured by a strict moral standard, we find these truths to be evident

At **Providence, *RI*; Pawtucket, *RI*; Fall River, *MA*; Springfield, *MA*; Bangor, *ME*, Portland, Worcester, *MA*; Northampton, *MA*; "Businessmen's Prayer Meetings" are in daily progress. At Worcester, the conversions in all denominations number between two and three hundred, and the number is increasing.** At **Portland**, among other things mentioned as pleasing instances of revival, a fire company has come within its influence, and taken two seats at one of the churches, in the name of the company, and that the rent of them was to be paid out of the funds of the company. Laboring men on their way to and from work at noon, stop in and take part for a few minutes in the exercises. In **Hadley, *MA***, the *Puritan Recorder* says the present exceeds even the "Great Revival of 1614 (?)." **Six hundred people have been converted in New Bedford, MA.**

In **Newark, NJ,** the union prayer meetings are attended to overflowing. Some of the stores in the chief business streets are closed, with a notice on the door: "Will reopen at the close of the prayer meeting." There is quite a religious interest among members of the Fire Department, and some of the engine houses will be shortly opened for prayer meetings.

At **Schenectady, it is said that there are two daily prayer meetings now established.** Converts have come in with surprising rapidity, many among the students in Union College. **The ice in the Mohawk has been broken on several occasions for the purpose of administering the ordinance of baptism by immersion.**

In the **Virginia** Conference of the Methodist Church, there are reported 857 accessions to the churches within the last few weeks; in the **Erie Conference over 700**; in the

Jamestown District more than 1,300; and in the Pittsburgh Conference more than 1,000.

A Legislative Prayer Meeting was instituted yesterday morning in the room of the Court of Appeals. It is to be continued every morning.
(The Troy Weekly Times., March 27, 1858)

1858–THE GREAT AWAKENING

The "Great Awakening," we are happy to say, still progresses; and there is no abatement in the manifestations of newly awakened zeal. In this city, the attendance at extra meetings continues large, and the number of conversions is highly gratifying to those who devote themselves to the good work.

In **West Troy, NY,** at the Methodist and Baptist churches, revived meetings still continue; and the idea of abandoning them which had been formed about two weeks ago, has been abandoned.

At **Saratoga, NY,** union prayer meetings are held, at which all denominations cordially unite.

In **Albany, NY,** among other novelties, a Legislative prayer meeting is in order; and a local paper wickedly suggests that it should "take effect immediately" in the hope that it might make a marked improvement in the morals of the Assembly.

We continue, as we shall every week during its prevalence, to give a synopsis of the leading facts and incidents of the revival: "Do you profess religion?" "No, sir, I profess my faith and practice my religion." Reader, go thou and do likewise.

It is stated that in one of the villages of the town of Simsbury, CT, there is not an adult to be found who has not been converted.

It is said that Mrs. Julia Dean Hayne, the actress, has joined the Episcopal Church in **California** and is now a regular communicant.

Over 6,000 maidens of the Sandwich Islands (*Hawaii*) have presented a beautifully bound copy of the Bible to their Princess.

Chapin, having said that he does not believe a sinner can he converted by a sudden shock, is asked what he thinks of the case of Paul the Apostle, as recorded in the New Testament?

The Rev. Mr. Seeley, American minister in Paris, is preaching in the Talbout Chapel, (*while*) waiting for the opening of the American Chapel, in that city, now shortly to take place.

Wm. Harrington, a notorious prize fighter, was converted at a recent meeting in **Newark, NJ**. He was heard to say before the meeting closed, "I have fought men all my life; the rest of it I will fight for Jesus."

Judging from the data afforded by the history of the revival operations which have hitherto prevailed and the general state of the public mind in this country, we can see no reason why the present Awakening should not extend over the whole land.

A noteworthy feature of the revival at **Hartford, CT,** is that prayer meetings have been held in several fire engine houses. The attendance has been large, the persons present being chiefly members of the companies.

The clergymen of **Chicago, IL,** propose a day of prayer that the consummation of the Kansas iniquity may be averted by divine providence, and that the President and his cabinet and Congress may be converted. A worthy object of Christian supplication.

The Philadelphia Ledger doubts the report that Edwin Forrest has become a Christian, but it believes if he has become a Christian, he will be a most zealous and devoted one, and if he is determined to be a Christian, all Beelzebub cannot stop him.

The **New York City** Temperance Alliance have published a card declaring that it is their belief that now is the proper time to affect a revival of Temperance Reform and asked for cooperation in their efforts to extend the principle of moral suasion (*persuasion*).

The citizens of **Taylor County, VA,** have held a public meeting, and resolved upon the condemnation of all the Christian Advocates published at the North, and the prosecution of all parties distributing them, in consequence of the Anti-Slavery sentiments they inculcate.

In a single building in **Boston, MA,** Thursday evening there was a prayer meeting on one floor, a boxing exhibition in the room above, and a Calico Ball in the upper hall. *(Women would sew calico dresses, wear them to the ball, and then later donate them to charity.)*

Theodore Parker, in a recent lecture, said he did not believe in the philosophy of this revival. He thinks it proceeds from a false idea of good and a fictitious enthusiasm that proceeds from sympathy, just as do Spiritualist, political, or temperance excitements. Meanwhile, the good people connected with the religious denominations of Boston are ceaselessly offering up their prayers for his conversion.

The tide rises in **New York City. There are meetings being held in no less than fifteen churches every day, as well as in Burton's Theatre.** Besides, tracts and placards are daily distributed, and Christians go from house to house to invite families to attend. On Sunday, the "Flying Artillery" took possession of the Seventeenth Street Methodist Church, and there were fifteen conversions during the evening meeting.

In the towns on the western border of Vermont, the work is SO general and remarkable as to attract the attention of all classes. It is not confined to the churches; hundreds are converted at prayer meetings, in private houses, in the workshops, and at their work in the fields. Neither is it confined to the vulgar; men of rank, fortune and fashion, lawyers, physicians, and respectable tradesmen, and indeed, all classes, ages, and sexes are the subjects of it.

A spirited revival is in progress at a disgraceful locality in **Boston** known as the "Black Sea." The services are conducted by Father Mason, the venerable city missionary. The attendance of abandoned men and women is very large, and it is wonderful to see what a respectful attitude of devotion they present. On Thursday afternoon, one touching appeal was made, with some apparent effect, to the degraded women present. The intemperate were earnestly addressed by two persons, one of whom has been a "fast" young man who said he had lived in sin some ten years, had spent $30,000, and had freely indulged in intoxicating drinks in fashionable places; but within a year his attention had been arrested by the Spirit of God, and he had been brought to repentance. He earnestly exhorted others to the Savior.

The late Rev. Dr. Harry Croswell, during his ministry of forty-one years as rector of an Episcopal church in **New Haven, CT,** baptized 2,553 persons, married 837 couples, and officiated alone at 1,844 burials.

At **Gardiner, ME, the Methodists are holding a protracted meeting and converts are rapidly falling in.**

New London, CT, is said to have been moved from center to circumference, **a daily union prayer meeting is held, and there have been some hundreds of conversions.** The most influential citizens are prominent in the work.

At **Saco, ME,** there have been about **100 conversions** including several prominent lawyers.

Greeley & Co., of *The Tribune,* announce that they will publish, on next Saturday, an eight-page extra sheet of their paper, devoted exclusively to a history of this great awakening, and the incidents connected therewith. The fact that such a popular publication is called for by popular demand, shows what a deep seeded interest there is in this revival.

There is a revival among the Catholics at **Burlington, VT,** as the result of a protracted meeting or "Spiritual Retreat," as they term it, recently held by four of the Redemptorist fathers. The largest church was crowded from day to day, and one of the good fruits of the work has been the abandonment of liquor selling by several penitent Irishmen. The French Catholics arc now cnjoying a "spiritual rctreat," undcr the direction of several priests from Montreal.

President Sterns of Amherst College, says that three-fourths of the students in that institution are pious, and conversions are rapidly going forward. In all the region around Amherst the good work was progressing, and sinners were converted. A young gentleman, well known in musical circles, arose and bore testimony to the love of Christ in the salvation of his soul. Last Thursday, he attended the meeting to see and laugh at them; God met him, and now he came to pray.

A great revival is in progress at **Circleville, OH,** where some **200** have joined the Methodists and a less number—the other churches; and the work still goes on.

The last two numbers of the *North Western Christian Advocate*, the Methodist paper for the North-West, have contained reports of nearly five thousand five of a protracted hundred conversions, and the same paper states that there have been not less than **40,000 accessions** to the Northern Methodist church since the beginning of the present year.

Here is what Henry Ward Beecher says: "Take a sharp-cut young saint, just crystalized, many pointed, and as clear as a diamond, and how good he is! How decided for the right, and how abhorrent for the wrong! He has not yet attained to the meekness and gentleness of Christ. For these graces, we must look to the aged saints, who have learned, through the experience of the years, to carry themselves always with tender sweetness, and who hang on the horizon of life as the summer sun sometimes hangs in the western sky, mellowing half a hemisphere with its radiance."

At **Newburyport, *MA*,** the revival has reached the lower strata of society. A gentleman there, residing near a house that has not borne the best character, where some half dozen or more females board, was alarmed a few evenings since, by loud outcries, and ran to the spot expecting to see evidence of violence or bloodshed, but was surprised as he approached, to find that the inmates were holding a prayer meeting; and while some had been converted, others were calling aloud for mercy and deliverance from sins.

The religious revival at **Albany, NY,** is now growing, if possible, more intense the present week, than it has been doing the past fortnight. **Each day, morning, noon, and night, the temples of religious worship are thronged with converts, the hopeful, and the unconverted, and those who are asking**

what they must do to be saved. The same feeling pervades all ranks and classes of men. All mingle as brethren together, the sons and daughters of a common Parent, whose glory alone they seek to proclaim.

The union of effort among Christians of all denominations is one of the most remarkable incidents of this revival. The walls of sectarianism have been broken down, and there is everywhere observable a united labor for good result. A change of heart, a change of purpose, a strengthening of the will to resist temptation, and pursue after what is for their eternal welfare, are the objects sought by those who throng the house of prayer. Let the skeptic and worldling question their sincerity or mock their devotions, if they will; but the serious and the good will rejoice at this awakening of the moral sensibilities and indulge the hope that it will yield great and beneficial results.

The Freeman's Journal, the Roman Catholic Organization at **New York**, in commenting on the revival, says: **"In these 'revival' meetings, laymen seem to be taking fully as active parts as clergymen. This may be a hint to us Catholic laymen, in our places, to remember that we too may, each one, be a missionary. No one of us ought to see any of our friends or acquaintances interested in seeking after matters of religion, without honestly, simply, and directly telling him of that truth which we possess, and which he will seek elsewhere in vain.** Grander means than these must be used to meet the full tone of public thought and sentiment. **We must have apostolic missionaries and priestly authority to convert the country; and a religious movement, such as at this time is spreading over the whole country, is an incentive to new exertions in this way—but at the same time, God may use the simplest means; and every Catholic, man or woman, should consider himself and herself a missionary."**

Among the converts at **New Bedford, *CT*,** where over **600 are numbered**, is a liquor dealer, who lately rose in a prayer meeting and avowed his determination never again to sell or drink a drop of liquor.

At **Mamaroneck, NY,** where **130 persons** have joined the Methodist church, a recently converted fisherman said: "When we used to go down to the creek to fish, we used to curse and use all sorts of profane language; but now we go out in our boats singing, and songs of praise are wafted from one boat to another."

The revival has extended as far South as **Mobile, AL,** where protracted meetings are held in all the churches.

All along the Hudson, the revivals continue, and there is scarcely a village in which converts may not be numbered by scores.

In **Newark, NJ,** over **3,000 conversions** have been made, and the feeling manifested is remarkable. Old men, who are but awaiting the coming of the chariot to bear them home, and young men who hope for opportunities in which to gather many sheaves in the garner, labor side by side; gratitude and faith are exhibited in every prayer and exhortation, and there is a community of feeling such as is seldom displayed, even among Christians.

The feeling is on the increase in **Philadelphia, *PA*.** The noon prayer meeting has outgrown Jayne's Hall, which will seat **2,500**; and Franklin Hall, the headquarters of the "Free Thinkers" and the infidels, has been obtained and opened as a place of prayer.

In some neighborhoods, almost the entire adult population is brought under its influence. In many churches, there are from **100 to 200 accessions**.

(**The Troy Weekly Times., April 03, 1858**)

CHAPTER 2

REVIVAL TRIVIA

The following articles and tidbits are amusing and interesting snapshots of revival-time history. Some are humorous and others have a very serious overtone, but I believe that you will find them interesting, nonetheless.

PREACHER PAID IN EGGS

Circuit Rider's Story Told at M. E. Conference, St. Louis

The hardships of a Methodist circuit rider were brought forcibly to the attention of the city ministers attending the St. Louis conference of the Methodist Episcopal Church when one country preacher reported that in the last two months he had received half of a hog and a great many eggs, but no money. He had sent twelve dozen eggs to the District Superintendent, he said. Another circuit rider said he had received $19 in two months, and a third *said* that he had received no money, but that his parishioners had promised to buy him a horse before winter and had entertained him liberally in their homes.

(The Nassau Post., November 05, 1915, Page 2)

At one of the New York theatre meetings, Rev. Sidney A. Corey, of the Fifth Avenue Baptist Church, said, "I must be pardoned if I refer today for half a minute only, to the emotions that swell my own bosom. Four years of my life was spent in the front of the footlights amidst scenery. In 1838, providentially called home to see an aged mother, I fell into the midst of just such a revival as there is in this great metropolis—desiring to tarry but a few days, and then return to a settled engagement I had in one of the theatres of this city. I was induced to hear a singular preacher while at home, for I had never been accustomed to attend church. I had been in the house but five minutes before the preacher, in the illustration of his subject, used this historical fact: **The bishop of London City sent to *David Garrick once, and asked him this question—** **'Mr. Garrick, how is it that you, in the development of fiction upon the stage, can overwhelm your entire audience, and can bathe them in tears, while I stand up to preach God's eternal truth to a sleepy congregation?' 'Oh, said the great Roscius of the English stage, 'I'll tell you; I'll tell you. You take God's truth and proclaim it as though it were fiction; we take fiction and present it as though it were truth.' 'That nailed me,' continued Mr. Corey, 'and I found no peace tilt I found it in the peace-speaking blood of the Lamb.'"**

Sadly, the same thing can be said about some churches today.

*David Garrick was an English actor and playwright who lived from February 19, 1717 to January 20, 1779.
(The Troy Weekly Times., April 03, 1858, Page 1)

———◆———

Old Bishop Aylmer, seeing his congregation pretty generally asleep, took his Hebrew Bible from his pocket and read a chapter, which roused attention, when the old minister sharply rebuked them for sleeping when they might have understood him and listening when they knew not a word he said.
(The Troy Weekly Times., April 03, 1858, Page 1)

———◆———

Among the gifts taken by the Prussian Prince to **England**, was a magnificent copy of Martin Luther's Testament, elegantly printed and bound, and so loaded with golden ornaments as to weigh twenty-seven pounds. It was given to the Bishop of London.

(The Troy Weekly Times., April 03, 1858, Page 1)

The African church at **Richmond, VA**, which has almost 3,000 communicants, has long been considered the largest congregation in the United States, but most yield that honor to the Methodist church in Beaufort, SC, of which J. M. C. Breaker is pastor. This clergyman writes to the Examiner: "I have baptized 585 persons in the fellowship of the Baptist church at this place (*Beaufort*), within the present year (*1857*), all of whom are colored, but eight; and this makes the present number of its membership 3,511—probably the largest church in the world. Of these one hundred are white, all the rest colored."

(The Troy Weekly Times., April 03, 1858, Page 1)

A revival is needed to burn up some things in the church. Not the old furniture, nor the dilapidated song books, nor faded carpets, but to burn up the spiritual idleness in the church, where many are doing nothing, and the bulk of the work falls on a faithful few.

(The Parisian., March 26, 1920)

Aroused pulpits will make aroused pews. Pulpits aflame will make pews aflame.

(The Sioux County Journal., December 20, 1894)

A noted gambler at **Uxbridge, MA,** has experienced a remarkable conversion. While sitting at the table with the cards in his hands, he was smitten almost like Saul of Tarsus. He could neither hold his cards nor play the game. His companions urged him to take another glass of liquor to quiet his nerves. He refused; and leaving them at their game, he started at once for home and found NO peace until he felt an inward evidence of forgiveness.

(The Troy Weekly Times., April 3, 1858)

ON THE TRAIL OF THE AMERICAN MISSIONARY
"Gift of Tongues" Given to Church in India

MAKING PRESBYTERIANS DANCE
(Small portion of a larger article)

…There has been a pronounced physical side to the demonstrations, as I found at Kedagaon. Entire audiences have shaken as if smitten with palsy, strong men have fallen headlong to the ground. **Even lepers have been made to dance. Leaping, shouting, rolling on the floor, beating the air, and dancing, have been common. Concerning dancing, Bishop Warne said, "Personally, I have not seen much of the dancing: that is reported as mostly having taken place in Presbyterian churches!" It is a fact that the dignified Presbyterians, even the Scotch church missions, have been foremost in these revival experiences.**

The revival has continued in various parts of the empire for more than a year; I have reports from Lucknow, Allahabad, Adansol, Moradabad, Bareilly, Khassia Hills, and Kedagaon. The Methodists baptized **1,900 new converts** during the year, besides the notable result of having secured more than **300 new candidates** for the ministry.

Dramatic in the extreme have been the confessions of sin and restitution, and therefore, the reconciliations between enemies.

Everywhere there is agreement that the lives of the people have been markedly altered for the better. "The revival," says one, "has given India a new sense of sin." The spontaneous composition of hymns has been a curious feature of some meetings. Bishop Warne thinks that "there will be a new hymnology in the vernacular as an outcome of this revival."

While columns more could be written concerning incidents of this revival, there is only room here to add that it must not be assumed that all of India is being stirred by these events. Many churches and missions are strangers to them, and the European population of the country as a whole knows nothing about them. Yet, it is the conviction of those who claim to have received the Pentecostal baptism that all of India is to be swept by a fire of religious revival. Some even say that they have been given direct, supernatural assurance of this fact.

(The Columbus Journal., January 01, 1908, Image 7)

REVIVAL IN WALES

Evan Roberts

It is difficult to explain psychologically the religious excitement now prevalent in Wales and in certain parts of Europe. Revivals in the past have usually occurred under the powerful stimulus of a great popular orator. For months before the revival began in Wales, ??? Torrey and Alexander were addressing large meetings in various parts of **Great**

Britain. The former is the preacher, the latter the singer. Like others before them, they are able to fill large auditoriums such as Albert Hall with masses of that robust nonconformist public, which is more emotional than the English are usually thought to be. The movement was planned and executed by these leaders, and so far as visible results to, it owes its success to them. **But the Welsh revival is different. It seems to be a spontaneous and ecstatic awakening of a whole people, irrespective of leaders and guides. Two leading ??? ministers who went down from London to attend the meetings could scarcely be persuaded to address an audience, for the people were conducting their own services; and while there was a great deal of praying and singing, there was little preaching.**

Evan Roberts, the nominal leader is not of the Wesley, the Whitefield, or even the Moody type. For a long time preceding the revival, he was in retirement to meditate and pray. Then he emerged to set in some mysterious way the ??? of his fellow countrymen on fire.

(The Evening Post: New York., March 6, 1905)

WHEN BAPTISMAL CEREMONY WAS A TRYING ORDEAL[1]

Description of Midwinter Baptisms in the Battenkill More than Eighty Years Ago

The following article descriptive of a baptismal scene in **Greenwich** many years ago is copied from a clipping from *The Washington County Post*. It was printed in that paper probably more than thirty years ago and gives an interesting description of the ceremony.

A Reminiscence

Many years ago, as you will perceive by the date—January 14, 1843, which was on Sunday, a young man who was learning the blacksmith's trade and working in a shop which stood near the Checkered House, was invited by his employer and his wife to accompany them to Greenwich to witness a baptizing. It was a very cold day and fine sleighing. When they arrived, they found a large concourse of people of all ages standing on the banks of the Battenkill awaiting the ceremony. Imagine the intense cold and the snow for a carpet around their feet; but the water flowed so swiftly there was very little ice on the river.

The minister, who was preaching at the Baptist Church at the time, was Elder Arthur, the father of Chester A. Arthur, who became the president after the assassination of James A. Garfield.

There had been wonderful protracted meetings (*many days, sometimes for weeks or months at a time*) **in the vicinity, especially at Cambridge, Center White Creek, and Greenwich**—*with* Elder Westcott helping the Baptist preachers and Rev. Brown at the Methodist churches. There was a large accession in the churches, especially *in* the Baptist Church at Greenwich.

At 10:30 or 11:00 a.m., the preacher, Elder Arthur, arrived at the riverbank fully equipped for his work, and the ceremony began. The people were led down into the water, one after another, the larger share being young men, until fifty were baptized, after which the preacher nearly dropped from exhaustion; but having recovered himself after a few moments, he said that if there were only two or three more to be baptized he thought he could hold out. So the baptizing went on until there were twenty more people led down into the water, making seventy in all. **Was not that a miracle as much as any of**

**which we read in the Bible? What ordinary man could have
endured such exposure and fatigue? Is it to be wondered at
that his son should live to fill the highest office in the land?**

The following Sunday the same young man borrowed
or hired a horse and cutter from a neighbor (Holden Wells by
name) and inviting his promised wife to accompany him, drove
to Greenwich to see the final end of the baptizing. The weather
was a little milder or it seemed so to him, being in such pleasant
company; and he was driving one of the best roadsters in the
vicinity, which was no small consideration to his mind.

When they arrived at the same place on the bank of the
Battenkill, the same Elder Arthur lead thirty-five more persons
down into the water in baptism, **making one hundred and five
as the fruit of that one revival for the Greenwich Baptist
Church**. That church is a strong church today, and who can say
with truth that revivals are a sort of insanity or frenzy similar to
kind of delirium tremens, as some of the learned scientists are
writing in the magazines of the day?

The young man who was witness of the incident here
related is Russell P. Twiss of Cambridge, and his fiancée was
Miss Pamelia Deuel, whom he married in November of the
same year.
**(The Greenwich Journal and Fort Edward Advertiser.,
November 30, 1927, Page 9, Image 9)**

HOT TIME AT CAMP MEETING

"Holy Roller" Tarred and Feathered
by Jay and Wilmington Men

There was a hot time at **Wilmington, *OH*,** on Friday
night at a camp meeting that was being held by members of the

"Holiness" sect, which seems to have quite a few advocates in the northern part of this state. **Followers of this peculiar belief are commonly called "Holy Rollers,"** and on several occasions, warm times have been experienced by them in seeking converts. A band of them had been holding meetings in a tent that they had pitched about two miles from Wilmington, and their customs and beliefs had been severely roasted by the people of that staid town. **The climax was reached Friday night when a crowd of men from Wilmington and Jay got together and taking one of the most prominent "Rollers," George Perry of Scioto, Clinton County, *OH*, gave him a coat of feathers.**
(**Ticonderoga Sentinel., September 26, 1907, Page 1, Image 1**)

"When the heart is right, the conduct is right. The problem is that we've been dealing with the conduct."—Billy Sunday

"Let God have a chance, and you will have the greatest revival you ever saw."—Billy Sunday

"A revival is the normal condition of the church. A lack of revival is abnormal."—Billy Sunday

"Everywhere that Paul went, he had a revival or a riot."—Billy Sunday
(**The Presbyterian of the South: Southwestern Presbyterian, Central Presbyterian, Southern Presbyterian., January 22, 1919, Image 2**)

SHAKEN BY EARTHQUAKES

Two shocks by earthquakes were felt at the South, in the West, and as far North as **Pittsburg, Cleveland, and Indianapolis**, soon after 1 o'clock on Monday afternoon. At the South, in **Maryland, Virginia, North Carolina, Georgia, and**

Tennessee, the shocks were quite severe and lasted, in some places, over two minutes. In **Virginia, near Parkersburg, there was caused a big fissure in the earth**; and in various places, bricks from chimneys were dislodged and pictures thrown from the walls. **The negroes, as usual, took the shocks very seriously; and a number of their preachers commenced revival meetings at once.**
(**The Columbia Republican.**, June 03, 1897, Page 2, Image 2)

Rev. Billy Sunday closed his great revival in **Scranton, PA**, last Sunday, after seven weeks of extraordinary religious manifestation. Nearly **18,000 persons professed conversion** and added their influence to the army that will fight the forces of evil in Pennsylvania. As a result of religious campaigns in the Keystone State, Billy Sunday has converted **75,000 persons during the past year**. He now goes to **Huntington, WV,** where he will hold a revival.
(**Shepherdstown Register.**, April 23, 1914, Image 2)

A Methodist revival at **Connersville, IN,** has resulted in **500 conversions** and is still in progress.
(**Semi-weekly Interior Journal.**, February 26, 1886, Image 3)

CHANGED HIS MIND

In a revival on **Mt. Elkhorn,** near the **West Virginia** line, there was a lively scene one night last week, according to a report from a correspondent in that locality. A protracted meeting had been in progress for two weeks, much to the displeasure of three of the hard characters in the neighborhood. The preacher was warned to leave. This, he persistently refused to do. On the night in question one of the worst mountain men went to the church in the middle of the service, and with pistol in hand, informed the minister that he must leave. The good, old fellow walked down the aisle and proceeded to give the coward a sound thrashing. Like a whipped cur, the desperado made tracks with the heels toward the meeting house.

(The Mt. Sterling Advocate., April 14, 1896, Image 2)

ALL NIGHT

PRAYER SERVICES TO BE HELD AT PRESBYTERIAN CHURCH ON NEW YEAR'S EVE

The United Prayer Band will hold a watch and prayer service New Year's Eve at the Presbyterian Church, commencing just after the church services and continuing until after twelve o'clock. **All those who desire to tarry in prayer for the rest of the night, that a general revival will spread throughout our land, are requested to stay at the close of the watch service.** All who are interested in a revival are most cordially invited to come and spend what time they can in this service.

(The Democratic Banner., December 29, 1916, Page 5, Image 5)

ARE REVIVALS OUT OF DATE?

After the death of Dwight L. Moody, many prominent clergymen in Chicago did not hesitate to say that the era of revivals had passed. They contended that Mr. Moody was the last of the great revivalists and that there was no demand for another.

This contention was based on the theory that people were less emotional than a generation ago, less inclined to impulsive action in religious matters, and more inclined to act deliberately on conviction. Therefore, old-fashioned preaching, that aroused or frightened people, had had its day.

In answer to this argument came the tour of the Rev. R. A. Torrey, the friend and associate worker of D. L. Moody. Mr. Torrey went as an evangelist to Australia and organized a campaign for the conversion of men and women, just as Moody had organized his revival campaigns in Chicago, New York, or London. He was as successful in this new field as Moody had been twenty years earlier in his greatest revival tour. Thousands were converted, and there was great revival of interest in religious work.

A tour in Europe and Asia followed, and Mr. Torrey returned with 30,000 converts to his credit and was welcomed to Chicago as the great revivalist of the time. Judged by the results of his work, he is.

On another page of this issue of the Sunday *Inter Ocean*, Mr. Torrey writes of his beliefs, of his plans, and of his experience abroad. He believes that in the future the revival is to play as conspicuous a part in the religious experience of the world as it has played in the past. He believes that his efforts have been successful, because he appeals to the conscience in the old-fashioned way.

He is a revivalist, pure and simple, an evangelist working to convert men by old-fashioned Gospel preaching; and he has had wonderful success. He is justified in his belief that the most effective way to bring people into the church is to preach the Gospel to them. His experience is standing testimony against the theory that revivals are out of date.
INTER OCEAN
(The Seattle Republican., July 10, 1903, Image 5)

A NEW STYLE OF CONVERTING SINNERS

To Build a Church on Wheels and Drive It Through the Country with Four Horses

CLYDE, NY

May 22—Mr. Osborn, the drummer evangelist, who has been holding revivals here, has devised a new plan of introducing the Gospel. **The idea of Mr. Osborn is to reach as many as possible of the class of people who do not attend church. He will build a large chariot and make a pilgrimage through the country. This church on wheels will be large enough to hold a company of sinners and a piano and will furnish a place from which the evangelist can address his audiences. It will go from town to town, drawn by four horses.** The drummer evangelist will receive financial backing from Mr. Sheldon, a wealthy resident of Auburn.

(The Portland Daily Press., May 23, 1895, Image 1)

CHAPTER 3

HUGE REVIVAL AT HOWES CAVE, NEW YORK–1880

Howe Caverns is now a famous tourist attraction that has hosted over 14 million people since it first opened to the public in 1929.[1] Imagine that just a few years earlier, in 1880, thousands gathered right nearby for a huge revival.

BAILEY'S GROVE—HOWES CAVE
(Howe Caverns)

The Albany District Camp Meeting will be held in Bailey's Grove, near Howes Cave, about the middle of August. Rev. J. E. C. Sawyer, Presiding Elder, will take charge. Every arrangement for the comfort of those who may attend is being made; a large fence encircles the whole encampment. For the free use of tent companies, a well-stocked icehouse has been put up on the grounds. A large stable for boarding horses is being erected. There will be reduced rates on the railroad, etc., etc. All pastors attending, also their horses, will be boarded free of charge. Further notice will appear hereafter.
(The Cobleskill Index., June 17, 1880, Page 3, Image 3)

CAMP MEETING

Camp Meeting at **Howes Cave, NY,** reached a culminating point last Sunday. **There are various estimates of the number of people present, most putting the figures at six**

or seven thousand. A person informed us that **at noon 1,200 vehicles had reached the grounds.** Perhaps as many more arrived after that hour. The woods literally swarmed with life. Many could only find accommodations for horses in barns located a long distance from the grounds. In one procession on the **Cobleskill Road,** there was an unbroken line of fifty vehicles. Some came in great loads before which four horses were harnessed; some lived in the immediate vicinity of the grounds, while many came from a very long distance in order to serve the Lord under great disadvantages.

The day was hot and the dust more than abundant. **The shuffle of thousands of feet ground the dust into the most minute particles, which arising, filled the air like a sort of vapor, which drifted to and fro. This dust settled upon the person and clothes. We noted many a fine silk dress upon which the genteel owner could easily have traced her name in the dust.**

That so very large a number should crowd around the preacher's stand and eagerly drink in the Gospel truths presented, speaks well for the religious devotion of the multitude. In the afternoon, the sermon was delivered by Rev. Mr. Thompson of Canajoharie. The speaker's form and voice were commanding, and his topic ably discussed. The preacher was followed by Rev. Mr. Ford, of Schenectady, in an exhortation that was a superior supplement to a masterly sermon.

The best of good order prevailed. But one slight disturbance occurred, and that was soon quelled. We did not see even one man drunk, and if there is any aggregate good in camp meetings, this must certainly have been fruitful of such results.

(The Cobleskill Index., August 26, 1880, Page 3, Image 3)

CHAPTER 4

MASSIVE REVIVAL IGNITES TICONDEROGA, NEW YORK—1915

Nestled at the base of the Adirondacks, Ticonderoga is a small town with a population of approximately 5,000 people. It is rich in Revolutionary War history and seems like an "unlikely" place for revival to break out, but in 1915, that's just what happened. There are many other "unlikely" places across the United States as well as in other parts of the world, but God doesn't see things the way that man does, and His will can be accomplished on the planet wherever there are willing, hungry hearts.

EVANGELICAL CAMPAIGN ENDS IN BLAZE OF GLORY

Converts Number 825

Nearly $1,000 Raised for Dr. Henry and His Associates

The evangelical campaign at **Ticonderoga, *NY*,** is now a part of history, though hardly a thing of the past. It still lives in the result attained which all observers, especially those from away, pronounce to be immense. The campaign closed Sunday night in a blaze of glory. The free will offering on Sunday was between $950 and $1,000. A goodly part of this sum goes to pay a portion of the salaries of the evangelical party—the balance to Dr. Henry.

The closing service of the campaign in the big tent Sunday night packed it to its capacity and bulged the walls trying to accommodate a **1,200 *person* audience** in a space estimated to hold a little over 1,100, but this crowding of the tent physically, was as nothing compared to the wonderful spirit that filled the place to overflowing and brought in power to this great gathering of people regardless of creed or church affiliation. The vital fact is that there in something definite and determining about the saving power of the Lord Jesus Christ in the lives of men and women, young and old, that must sooner or later be recognized by each individual desiring to live up to the full measure of life's possibilities here on earth even if they do not grasp its significance as a dominating influence as to their connection with the great beyond.

Never in Ticonderoga and possibly never in Northern New York has such a great spiritual quickening been experienced as that brought to this town and vicinity by this campaign. Through it all ran the high plane of method and conduct rigidly adhered to by Dr. Henry and his party in their evangelistic work. **Free from all emotionalism and buffoonery, Dr. Henry has presented the solid meat of Biblical truths to his hearers in a manner scholarly and dignified in marked degree, but with an appealing force that carried by its powerful logical conviction to many a man and woman, boy and girl who had never made the "Great Decision" and brought them courageously out into an open confession of Jesus as Savior and King.**

These "Great Decisions" have come from no one walk or condition in life but have exemplified the wide reach of the saving power of God's love as applied to the human family. The

825 open confessions that have come as a direct result of these meetings are only a part, possibly the smaller part of the great blessing that has come to this community. There is a stirring toward higher ideals of life and living in the lives of many who are yet in the valley of indecision, and there in an awakening of the Civic Conscience, and a sense of individual responsibility has also appeared, that unless all signs fail, will place Ticonderoga and its neighboring town to the north definitely and permanently in the dry column on Nov. 2nd.

The three great services of Sunday totaled an attendance of nearly **3,600 people** in the big tent, not a few coming a distance of over a hundred miles to be present.

The morning topic of Dr. Henry was "God's Great Blockade to a Lost World."

The attendants at the afternoon meeting were privileged to hear Dr. Henry give his "Ten Reasons Why Every Man Should Vote Dry" and to hear Mr. Van Camp sing "The Twin Ballots" and "The Brewer's Big Horses" and to sing themselves, led by the chorus and Van Camp, "John Barleycorn, Goodbye!" At its close was witnessed one of the greatest temperance demonstrations ever seen in the Champlain Valley when the entire audience, including over 500 men, rose as one person and with uplifted hands pledged themselves in the matter of carrying Ticonderoga for no-license "to See This Thing Through."

The closing service at night was the largest held during the campaign, filling the big tent until standing room only would have been at a premium had it not been for the large supply of extra chairs to draw on from the Methodist church social rooms, adjoining.

Dr. Henry spoke on the topic, "The Halfway House," where many who have felt the quickening of their spiritual life under the inspiration of God's truths, having never arrived at The Great Decision, remain perhaps all their lives, never reaching the promised land and great blessing of any open confession of Jesus as their Savior and King.

In response to Dr. Henry's appeal at the close of the message, nearly thirty persons made open and definite confession of their acceptance of Jesus Christ and their determination to lead a Christian Life.

Resolutions were adopted by a unanimous standing vote, presented by F. B. Wood, chairman of the Executive Committee. The resolutions were an acknowledgement of the success of the work and included thanks to all who had taken part in the work.

Dr. Henry left on the midnight train for New York and Philadelphia, where Mr. Robinson had preceded him some days ago. Mr. and Mrs. Van Camp and their son, "Billy," go to **Keeseville** by auto, where the entire party opens a campaign on Wednesday.

Their going from Ticonderoga and leaving the many warm friends they have made during their stay here, strikes the only note of sadness in the entire campaign, which leaves this old town aglow with a friendliness and good cheer that are not the least of the blessings that their ministrations in the Providence of God have brought.

(Ticonderoga Sentinel., October 14, 1915, Pages 1 & 5)

Dr. Henry's Subject Last Night was "The Devil's Mortgages"

Devil's Mortgages on State and Individual Are Told

"The Devil's Mortgage on Ticonderoga" was the theme handled by Dr. Henry at last night's tent meeting. He took for his text the words of St. Paul to the Romans, "I am carnal, sold under sin." He said that these words applied to backsliders as well as to the lost in general.

He spoke first of mortgages on city, state, and national government, going into particulars in regard to three. The first, he said, is the liquor traffic, the mortgage being its licensing by the various forms of government.

The second mortgage, the evangelist said, is partisan politics. He said that the time has come when the good of man should be sought and that parties should be supported only when they minister to this end.

The third mortgage is that of criminal and undesirable aliens. "Immigrants have made contributions to the brawn and brain of our people," said the evangelist, "and also to our moral and spiritual force, yet not all are of this sort. About two-thirds of all crime is committed by the one-sixth who are foreign born."

"Not even the churches are free from Satan's mortgages, for through rationalized ministry and a secularized laity, he has fastened his clutches upon these organizations. Higher criticism has awakened the faith of many, and the worldly spirit in the church has helped the devil in keeping many from paying attention to the message of the churches.

"Individual souls are also under mortgage to the devil. Paul was speaking for himself in the text. One lien he enforces is sordid self-indulgence as in the case of the drunkard, the gambler, the cruel, the wicked, all of whom are selfish. Worldly pleasure also binds many to evil. Amusement is good, but it should be helpful, not harmful. Moral cowardice also ties others to Satan. **We have a generation of moral mollusks, spiritual** invertebrates, with a wishbone instead of a backbone. Indifference is another lien the devil holds on different ones—people who know but who will not act."

Dr. Henry grew more earnest as he laid stress on the fact that there is no future with God, that now is the only time with him, and that all these mortgages are due at this very moment. He also showed that men have nothing to pay; in their own strength, men cannot satisfy the mortgages that are upon them.

"How glorious it is," he declared, "that the Gospel tells of a Christ who pays it all. The one who is sold under sin is made free by the precious blood of Christ.

"Heaven is full of cancelled mortgages, freeing the souls of those who have been under sin, mortgaged to sin, death and Satan."

The subjects for tonight and succeeding meetings are:
Thursday evening—Blowing Up the Hell Gate of Sin.

Friday: 3:00 p.m.—Vision and Victory; 7:30 p.m.—Haunted Homes. A great family night.

Saturday: 3:00 p.m.—Paying the Fiddler; 7:30 p.m.—Young men especially should hear this.

Sunday: 10:30 a.m.—Unfurling the Flag of Faith; 3:00 p.m.—The European Slaughterhouse or What This Awful War is Doing; 7:30 p.m.—The Unpardonable Sin.

Will the campaign succeed? Is the Gospel still a power? Is the Christian religion still a vital force? Is there power in prayer? Does the community want improved conditions? Do individuals recognize their need of spiritual power in daily life?

All these and many other questions are being affirmatively answered in the big tent meetings on West Exchange Street, being conducted by J. Q. A. Henry and Jesse Van Camp. That changed lives would result under the ministry of Dr. Henry was a foregone conclusion, but the remarkable response indicates that a deep spiritual awakening is sure to result both in the cooperating churches and throughout the community. Nearly one hundred have already "hit the sawdust trail," and that after only one week's meeting.

Dr. Henry's preaching is strong, sane, and spiritual. His command of language, his illustrations, and his positive sincerity never fail to leave his hearer thoughtful. That a rising tide of enthusiasm with corresponding results will be the outcome is the general anticipation.

"The town is being moved and men are thinking as never before. It means great things for Ticonderoga."—Forest B. Wood

"The presentation of the ideals of good citizenship and Christian service, as made by Dr. Henry from day to day, cannot but have a good effect on the community."—W. A. E. Cummings

"I certainly think the campaign now in progress will benefit Ticonderoga and vicinity. I believe it should have the support of every moral and Christian force in the town."—R. J. Bryan

The evangelic campaign brings to Ticonderoga the opportunity of hearing one of the greatest evangelistic preachers of our day. There is nothing sensational in his preaching or methods.

Dr. Henry is a strong preacher. His sermons are thoroughly Christo centric in structure and tone, and deliverance with such religious unction that the judgement of the hearer is convinced and his heart moved. He believes in the Salvation of the Human Race through Jesus Christ. He is biblical in spirit and soul, with a high tide of spiritual life that lifts the soul of his hearers to a sacred nearness to God.

Mr. Van Camp, the soloist of the party, cannot be left out. He possesses a voice rich in tone and as clear as crystal; he sings with his soul; his enunciation is perfect; he sings his message sweetly and tenderly, and moves his hearers to tears. Not only does he sing, but he knows how to make others sing, which is a great gift. Mr. Van Camp has a very pleasing personality, and like Dr. Henry, is loved by all.

"I predict great success for the campaign. Let Ticonderoga awake and give God a chance."—Thomas de Gruchy.

"I think the campaign will mean a great moral uplift in the community."—G. H. Adkins.

"The evangelistic campaign is just what we need in Ticonderoga, and I think the final outcome will be a blessing to the people and an uplift to the whole community."—O. C. Badger.

"I think it's fine. Best thing that ever happened to Ticonderoga."—John Hennessey

Pen Points

A big **delegation from Hague, *NY,*** will visit the tent on Friday evening.

Rev. Blackmer of **Crown Point, *NY,*** is a regular nightly attendant.

Rev. Lewis of Crown Point, *NY*, arrived late for the Sunday evening service. The motor ran out of gasoline. Mr. Lewis and wife, with true perseverance of the saints, walked in from Streetroad.

Prayer Gatherings

Prayer meetings everywhere indicate the deep spiritual undertone behind the campaign meetings. Before each evening service, a prayer service is held at 7:00 and 10:00 a.m. daily in a number of private homes. Mrs. Mary Abbott has charge of these arrangements and will welcome invitations to hold such gatherings. A leader will be provided where necessary.

Music in the Tent

The people laugh, smile, shout, and then sing under the compelling leadership of Van Camp. As a leader of song, he is a wonder, and his solo work is simply thrilling. With a growing chorus choir, the music is providing a big attraction. Many catchy new choruses are on everybody's lips. "Brighten the Corner Where You Are" is very popular and "If You Win a Soul for Jesus, You Will Outshine the Sun" is a new and winning melody.

Humor

Inspiration and sympathy radiate from the leader's countenance as, in a homely Southern drawl, he "jollies" the crowd into responding. Mrs. Van Camp ably assists at the piano.

Quiet Hour Service

What may in many respects be considered the most important of services is the Evangelistic Company. Dr. Henry, during his several pastorates, was very successful in building up an active church membership because of his unusual ability to educate his helpers. The quiet hour services to be held on Tuesday, Wednesday, Thursday, and Friday afternoons of next week will be on the work and workings of the Holy Spirit. Christians are especially invited. Bring your Bibles.

(Ticonderoga Sentinel., September 23, 1915, Page 5, Image 5)

CHAPTER 5

EVANGELISTS' PERSPECTIVES

It is interesting to get the perspective of some of the great men and women of God who He used powerfully in the past. We can learn from their successes as well as their failures, and we can glean from the wisdom that they carried.

"He that walketh with wise men shall be wise:" Proverbs 13:20

WHAT THE EVANGELISTS SAY

If you ask one of the evangelists who are making big success in the revival field for the cause of the present movement, he will tell you that it is answer to prayer.

REVEREND A. C. DIXON—1907

This is what Rev. A. C. Dixon said: "We, who believe in the efficacy of prayer, believe that God is answering the petitions that have been going up for ten years all over the earth for a world-wide revival of religion. Although the non-church population does not know it, the fact is that Christians for a decade have prayed persistently, earnestly, and confidently for just such a movement as is now in progress. We are still praying, and the movement is increasing. How much stronger it will get only God knows.

"But I realize this answer will not satisfy those who do not believe in prayer. The unchurched, while forced by what they see to admit the strength and scope of the present revival movement, demand other reasons for its existence. And there probably are other reasons. **History shows us that faith comes in waves.** For some years, we have had higher criticism and educational force destructive of faith in the Bible. Dr. Briggs in the east, Dr. Harper of the University of Chicago in the west, the leaders of the Welhausen-Grafft school in Germany, and many others who have been in the front of the higher criticism movement have done much to destroy faith. But there is a swinging back from this fad. Darwinism is on the wane. These things seem to come in cycles, but **each wave of faith in the Bible that appears is much stronger than its predecessor, and in the end faith must triumph.**"

REV. MR. SUNDAY'S VIEW—1907

"Billy" Sunday has some very material reasons for the strength of the present movement. Here they are: "The plan of gathering together great audiences under one roof is one source of success. There is enthusiasm in numbers. Formerly, they tried to convert a town by holding revival meetings in a church that would not seat one-fiftieth of the population. Most of the successful revivalists insist nowadays on the erection of a tabernacle big enough to hold thousands, if there is not such a building already in town. And people now are so prosperous that they freely give money for this purpose where they formerly would not, but *in* back of it all is prayer. The scoffers deny this, but if a large number of scoffers were to ask a human power to give them a certain thing, in a certain way, at a certain time, and they received this thing, they would be pretty likely to think it came from the power they petitioned for it, even if they could not actually see it given."

(The Columbus Journal., April 03, 1907, Image 3)

REVEREND G. W. CROFTS—1888

WHAT IS A REVIVAL?

At the Congregational Church yesterday, **Rev. G. W. Crofts, the pastor, gave some very practical thoughts on revival movements**—the theme being suggested by the beginning here of a series of union revival meetings in this city. Mr. Crofts is evidently heartily in favor of a revival and spoke very earnestly of the need and desirability of such a movement. He spoke of the true revival not being a revival of sectarianism. He believed in sect and denominations. While such differences had at times led to foolish strifes over non-essentials, yet Christians were fast learning that, **while there might be an honest difference in heads, the hearts could be in close sympathy. All should be working for the same result, but a difference in methods and in organization was necessary to allow men to work best in accordance with their own peculiarities.** The true revival was not a revival of dogmatism. The speaker alluded to the prejudice felt among many good people against revivals because of the tendency to fanaticism. There was some ground, also, for this hesitancy about encouraging revival movements. There had been revivals of fanaticism, but a revival of religion was different entirely. While man's emotional nature should be recognized and used for good, the emotional should always be kept subject to the rational. **A fire which simply blares up, only to speedily die into a chill all the worse by the sudden contrast, was not the warmth which the heart of man needed. There should be the steady glow.**

The revival of religion was the turning of the hearts of men toward God, inspiring them into better living. Such a revival was desirable. It bettered not only the morals of individuals, but of the community. It was a work of *training* men to live in this world and preparing them for the world beyond. Such a revival should receive the help of every

Christian. All should give it active support. **God would do his part and keep his promises, but the work must be done through human agency.** The speaker strongly urged all to join in the work just started.

(The Omaha Daily Bee., November 26, 1888, Page 6)

BILLY SUNDAY—1915

"You can tell when a town needs a revival when Christians are willing to let God go ahead as He sees fit, and when these Christians will not balk at His orders to get out and work personally. We are only the earthen vessels for these revival fulfillments. **It is a great honor to be ambassadors for God. If God should send His Son to this town, and He should ask, 'Do you want a revival? Are you willing to let Me promote it as I see fit?' There would be the greatest stirring up this city has ever seen and the biggest religious awakening.**"

(Spoken by: Evangelist Billy Sunday—September 1915)

BILLY SUNDAY
ON THE REVIVAL IN WALES—1915

Day of Revival Is Not Over

"**Men say the day of the revival is over.** Fellows harp on that in the Methodist conference. In the Presbyterian meetings, in the Baptist associations, in the Congregational associations, the day of revival is over. **No, it is not. No, only with the fellow who vomits out the sentiment; but it is not over with God. Their day of revival is over.** God Almighty leaned over the battlements of heaven and looked down into the coal mines of Wales and said, 'Oh, Roberts!' and out of the depths of the coal mine came that grimy, soiled man, with dirty face, with a little lamp in his cap; and he said, 'What is it, God?' and God said, 'I want you to go and shake up Wales,' and he gave Wales the greatest revival that ever swept over this land since the days of Pentecost. There was not a college professor or preacher in Wales that God would trust with the job. 'The days of revival are over,' they said. Then God called Tony Alexander and told him to go, and he went to **Tasmania (*Australia*), Ireland, Japan, China, England, Scotland;** he went around the world."

(**Omaha Daily Bee., September 08, 1915, Page 2**)

Chapter 6

Miscellaneous Revivals

I don't believe that there is any location in the United States that has not been touched in some way by revival and awakening at some point in history. Listed here are just a few examples of long-since-forgotten past moves of God.

BRINKLEY, AK

GREAT THRONGS AT REVIVAL

Hundreds Attend Each Day

Evangelists Say that Signs Point to Great Revival in Brinkley

Every day at 2:30 in the afternoon and each night at 7:30, great throngs of people are in attendance at the revival meetings in the big brick warehouse on South New Orleans Avenue.

The Evangelists, Burke and Hobbs, say that there is every indication of this meeting being the greatest that they have ever held in Arkansas; and inasmuch as they have witnessed as many as **700 conversions** in some of their Arkansas meetings; this means much.

Many strong men and women have been influenced to join the Christian forces through this meeting, and many more are in regular attendance.

(**The Brinkley Argus.**, February 23, 1912, Image 1)

BURLINGTON, VT

Burlington, VT, has just experienced the greatest revival campaign it has known in 30 years. The campaign closed with a great meeting at the armory, which was packed to overflowing, even standing room being taken. The revivalists were Rev. Dr. Chapman and Mr. Alexander, the singing evangelist; and the meetings lasted 13 days. The churches there have received a great awakening. Hosts of young people joined the **Pocket Testament League** for a greater and more thorough reading of the Bible.

(**Ticonderoga Sentinel.**, December 3, 1908)

The Pocket Testament League is still in existence today, and you can go to their website and order up to 30 free Gospels of John every month. Over 100 million pocket-sized Gospels have been shared by members of this organization. www.ptl.org

---

ELLENBURGH DEPOT, NY

The Holiness Camp Meeting in session here the past week closed Tuesday night. The attendance throughout has been good, and last Sunday brought together the largest number we have ever witnessed here at a Gospel meeting, especially in the afternoon, when probably **800 people** were in attendance, many of whom drove 15 to 90 miles to the meeting.

(**The Plattsburgh Sentinel.**, September 03, 1897, Page 8)

FAIRHAVEN, MA

The Holiness camp meeting at Fairhaven, (*MA*), last Sunday drew some 5,000 people.
(Plattsburgh Republican., September 26, 1885, Page 1, Image 1)

GLENS FALLS, NY

GLENS FALLS—THE REVIVAL

The religious movement among the different denominations, inaugurated with the week of prayer, seems but very little abated. The Methodists closed their meetings the week before last; and the closing service, as a special effort with the Baptists was held on Friday evening of last week. After the sermon, four received the ordinance of baptism, making in all forty-four whom the Great Reaper has gathered in during this harvest season. Several more are waiting to be baptized, while others are anxiously inquiring, "'What shall I do to be saved?" Sunday was a day of great interest and rejoicing to them. It was communion season, and the whole number of those that had been baptized during this revival received the hand of fellowship. It was very impressive to witness this beautiful ceremony, as their pastor welcomed these new-born souls into the church militant. There has been a fresh interest manifested among Presbyterians of late, and quite a number of young men from that society have been led to see the reasonableness of religion.
(The Troy Weekly Times., March 15, 1873, Page 3)

GLOVERSVILLE & JOHNSTOWN, NY

Camp Meeting at **Cayadutta Park**. The A. M. E. Zion Churches of **Johnstown and Gloversville** will hold camp meeting services at Cayadutta Park Sunday, the 11th inst. Rev. J. E. Mason, D.D., of Rochester, and Rev. Washington Thompson, the old-fashioned camp meeting preacher, will be the speakers. The electric railroad will sell reduced round-trip tickets to the park for Sunday. Everybody is invited to attend the meetings.

(The Daily Leader., August 09, 1895, Page 8)

The camp meeting which began yesterday at **Cayadutta Park** under the auspices of the, A. M. E. Zion Churches of **Gloversville and Johnstown had an attendance of about five hundred persons during the day**, which certainly was very encouraging as a starter. Rev. R. M. Turner of Gloversville preached in the afternoon to an interested audience. Rev. B. W. Swain of Johnstown preached in the evening, also to a fine congregation. Good *order* and quietness prevailed. The song services were conducted by the members of the Gloversville and Johnstown choirs. The collections for the day were exceedingly light, and as money is needed to honorably meet the expenses of the churches, it is to be hoped that the camp meeting goers will contribute largely to help these, our worthy neighbors and friends. Rev. L. E. Mason, P. E., of Rochester, and Rev. G. J. Cliff of Amsterdam are booked for next Sunday.

(The Daily Leader., July 26, 1896, Page 8)

GRANVILLE, NY

EVANGELIST SHELDON HOLDS FIRST REVIVAL MEETING AT BIG TABERNACLE

Evangelist H. D. Sheldon arrived in Granville Wednesday evening accompanied by Mr. and Mrs. H. C. Mosher who have charge of the music in the meetings. Mr. Sheldon and his associates went directly to the Big Tabernacle on East Main Street and held the first service of Granville's revival campaign. The speaker held his audience in rapt attention, and the intense interest manifested in his words and message give promise of great times in the splendid building provided by willing hands and loyal hearts.

The services are to continue for five weeks, and at the end of that time, it will no doubt be apparent that many who are today indifferent to the claims of God upon the life have found a Savior, Friend, and Guide in the Christ of Calvary, and a church home whose spiritual help and counsel may be had continually. Special services will be announced from the platform and through the paper—for young people, men only, women only, for the children, and various organizations.

All the churches will unite in worship at the Tabernacle next Sunday morning when Mr. Sheldon will speak, 10:30 being the hour. The Sunday evening service will attract large crowds, and those not wishing to stand will need to arrive early, although seats have been provided for 1,500 or more people.

(The Granville Sentinel., November 19, 1915)

McCOMB, MS

REVIVAL MEETINGS CLOSED WEDNESDAY

Evangelist Culpepper and Singer John Robinson Leave for McComb

350 Proclaim Allegiance with God

All Churches Receive Portion of Converts

The big revival closed Wednesday night, which is said to be one of the most successful revivals ever held in this city. The Evangelist, Burke Culpepper of Memphis, TN, with Mr. John U. Robinson doing the singing, has done a great good for Water Valley. They came here and started the revival at the First Methodist Church June 8, but the crowds soon grew too large for the church; and it was found necessary to have a large tent, which was placed on what is known here as the government lot, just south of the First Methodist Church where **thousands of people** heard Evangelist Culpepper daily until the close of the revival last night. The revival was really a union revival, as all denominations took part in the services both morning and evening—in personal work and the song service. All denominations are largely benefited by this revival, as well as practically every person in the city. Rev. Culpepper preached about eighteen days, preaching about forty-five sermons; and there were a little over two hundred songs during this revival; and **about 45,000 people heard Evangelist Culpepper during this revival**. The conversions and reclamations are about three hundred and fifty, and most of them will connect themselves with one of the churches here. Possibly, a vast majority of them will go to the churches of their choice next Sunday. Among the personal workers, and one who did some remarkable work, was James Culpepper, son of the Evangelist who did a great work among the young people. James is about eighteen years of age and went right into the work almost like an old head who had many years of experience, and his efforts were not in vain. He caused many young people to go up and ask for the prayers *from* the Evangelist, and many of them gave their hearts to the Master. Evangelist Culpepper has added many divine thrills to the hearts of the people of Water Valley. He, his son, and Mr. Robinson left on train No. 6 last night for Memphis, where they will rest for a few days; and then they will go right into another meeting in McComb City, MS, next Sunday.

(**The North Mississippi Herald.**, June 29, 1923, Page 1)

NEBRASKA

For the benefit of those of our readers who are not subscribers to *The Daily*, we'll say that the union revival meetings have created a great interest already in the surrounding country. **The local attendance of the meetings up to date is estimated to be between 8,000 and 9,000—total number of converts to date, 114.** We believe that the readers of the weekly paper who are interested in the meetings will feel that they should be subscribers to *The Daily*.

(**The Alliance Herald.**, March 28, 1912, Image 1)

PATTERSON, NJ

Billy Sunday has just started a whirlwind six weeks' campaign for souls in **Paterson, NJ**. "There is not a city in the United States in greater need of revival," Sunday declared after looking over the ground. **The tabernacle specifically constructed in Paterson for the revival holds 10,000 people.**

(**The Arizona Republican.**, April 11, 1915, Page 7)

POTSDAM, NY

MASS MEETING SUNDAY

Rev. Milton Rees Addresses Magnificent Audience

Rev. Milton S. Rees opened union revival services at Potsdam Sunday at 3 p.m. in the Presbyterian church at a mass meeting for men. **Over three hundred men were in attendance**, and it is thought that not one was sorry for having been there. Mr. Rees is a man who knows men and knows how to appeal to them in a straightforward, manly style that brings about results. **He speaks from large experience of the personal kind and does not seek after sensational, "Clap Trap" methods but reaches his end by a manly talk of man to man.** His subject was "Mans Greatest Problem," and this he claimed to be. "What shall ye do with Christ?" As a helpful and uplifting address, the one on Sunday afternoon was exceptional. Mr. Rees speaks to "men only" again next Sunday at 3 p.m. in the same place. The subjects of his other meetings throughout the week and the place and time of holding the same may be found under church notes.

(Herald Recorder., October 28, 1906)

PRESCOTT, AR

INTERESTING REVIVAL

…In order that the businessmen and their employees may attend the informal social hour given Evangelist Earnest House (*of Topeka, KS*) who is conducting the revival at the Christian Church, all business houses in Prescott will close at six o'clock Friday evening. The patrons of our stores are requested to give their orders early in the afternoon Friday.

(The Nevada County Picayune., August 22, 1913, Image 1)

Wouldn't it be amazing if businessmen and businesswomen recognized the importance of revival today? What would happen if businesses closed early to allow men and women to meet for prayer?

SARATOGA, NY

The Methodist Church in **Saratoga, NY**, is enjoying a revival season. **The number of different persons who have been forward for prayers up to Sunday night, was 269; hopeful conversions, about 175; admitted to the church on probation, about 100.**

(The Plattsburgh Sentinel., April 17, 1868, Page 3)

TRUTHVILLE, NY

REVIVAL MEETINGS BEING HELD

Revival meetings are being held at the Baptist church this week. Rev. Mr. Miller of the western part of the state is in charge and is being assisted by Mr. Snyder, a singer. Excellent preaching is heard, and the meetings are very interesting. Come and help with your presence and interest.

(The Whitehall Times., January 15, 1914)

The greatest revival spirit in this country appeared in its most distinct form soon after the wonderful successes of Torrey and Alexander in England. **New England,** cold temperamentally and rock-bound religiously, cast off its traditional reserve and laid itself open to the influences of the "old-time" religion. In **Boston,** the evangelistic work under Rev. A. C. Dixon and others resulted in an unprecedented number of conversions. All over Canada, the same was true. **A** four weeks' campaign in Toronto, Canada, by Torrey and Alexander, resulted in 4,300 conversions.

Philadelphia, PA, next was attacked by the evangelists, and the enthusiasm whipped to a high pitch, *with* a small army of men, women, and children professing conversion. Every section of the country, outside possibly of the Pacific coast, has fallen under the wave of religious enthusiasm.

(The Columbus Journal., April 03, 1907, Image 3)

SYRACUSE, NY

A great religious revival is in progress in **Syracuse**. With services in the two churches and the Alhambra last Sunday, it is estimated that **15,000 persons** heard Rev. Dr. J. Wilbur Chapman, the revival leader, and his assistants.

(Mexico Independent., January 31, 1906, Page 6, Image 6)

CHAPTER 7

WHO WAS EVANGELIST W. E. GEIL?

In my research, I discovered that there are many little-known evangelists who made a big difference for the Kingdom of God in past revivals. As you'll see as you read the following newspaper clippings, Evangelist W. E. Geil was one such man!

WHITEHALL, NY

CONTINUES THE GOOD WORK

The many friends of Rev. W. E. Geil, in this vicinity, will read with pleasure the following from **Whitehall (*NY*)**: The most phenomenal revival work has been done in this village in the past ten days, during which Evangelist W. E. Geil has been conducting meetings. The largest building in town has been filled to overflowing daily and nightly; 500 people were converted; and the most intense interest was maintained. **All the business houses, including fifteen saloons, have been closed every evening at 6:45; and people generally have united in the work.**

(The Daily Republican., March 25, 1895)

POUGHKEEPSIE, NY

The successes and disappointments attendant upon the recent evangelistic services conducted by W. E. Geil were clearly pointed out by Rev. W. B. Hill in his discourse on Sunday evening. "In many ways, it has been of lasting benefit," said the speaker in referring to the revival, **"We have had a new training in Christian unity. All denominational lines were ignored from the outset, and at the close, there was no selfish scramble to bring converts into some particular church. We have also been roused to work."** Mr. Geil said truly that there would be no reaction after he left. All the churches in one way or another are seeking to continue evangelistic efforts. **The Christians have learned the pleasure of soul-winning and are desirous to have it henceforth. Then again, they have been trained to work. Some who never before offered a prayer in public have been taught to do so. Many who thought Christian visiting an impossibility have found it easy and delightful.** Cottage prayer meetings will henceforth be a regular part of church work in churches, which *have* never tried them before. And we must not forget that, though all whom we hoped to see brought to Christ were not reached, yet many were; and the salvation of a single soul is of infinite value in the sight of our Lord. More and more, it may be, as the days go by, we shall recognize that a good work has *been* wrought in our midst this winter—not altogether in the way we prayed for and expected, effectual in the building up of Christ's Kingdom among us and within us.

(**The Pokeepsie Evening Enterprise., February 24, 1896, Page 8**)

GLOVERSVILLE, FULTON COUNTY, NY

A STUPENDOUS WORK

**Accomplished Here in the Cause of Christianity
The Religious Fervor of the Past Two Weeks Unparalleled
in the Whole History of the Place**

Hundreds Have Pledged Themselves to Christ

The Men's Meeting Yesterday was a
Tremendous Gathering and an Inspiring Sight

A man skeptical as to the reality of Christianity must have been puzzled yesterday. It was evident the people of this city were contemplating religious things. The different churches were well filled in the morning, notwithstanding the fact that the people had been attending meetings nightly for more than two weeks, many of them staying until a late hour. In the afternoon, the streets were black with men making their way to the Baptist church, where a crowd assembled waiting for the opening of the doors. At three o'clock the great house presented a sight never to be forgotten. It was simply full. Hundreds stood throughout the long service. The choir and the pulpit were crowded, and the baptistry was filled. Fully 1,700 men faced the evangelist who fearlessly, in clean cut Anglo-Saxon, told them the truth. "Personal Purity" was the subject, and it was handled manfully by one who knows men and knows the secret of the appalling physical and moral degradation everywhere abounding. Mr. Geil has not delivered a more important or telling discourse. It was well received and will do untold good.

Four churches could hardly accommodate the crowds who in the evening assembled to hear the final sermon of the evangelist, who, notwithstanding the fact that he had done two men's work for a fortnight, spoke with freshness and power at each place. His closing words were very tender. Very modestly, he attributed the great results, not to himself, but to the personal workers, who, in the meetings and on the streets, have sought to gain men to Christian life and entreated them not to lay down this work. He spoke feelingly of his early life, which seemed to have had its full share of adversity, and of the work to which he has been called and in which he has been engaged for a comparatively short time. He gave stirring advice to the converts, who, with deep emotion, hung upon his words; and then, with the most successful after meeting of the whole series, his work came to an end.

1,200 ACCEPTED CHRIST

His coming has been a blessing to this city. About **1,200 people** have pledged themselves in audible prayer and by signing a card, to lead a Christian life. A large number are men, some of whom had wandered very far from the right. Entire families have been converted. Influences have been set in motion which will never cease in their operation. Christians have been led to see that personal work is the secret of success in enlarging the church and that everyone can do that work. They have learned that men are approachable and waiting to be helped. They have received a great uplift for themselves, and purpose to be more than they have ever been to the kingdom of the Perfect Man.

People who have not attended these meetings have been influenced by them. There has been a religious atmosphere. Not one arrest has been made since the work began. The people who criticized at the beginning have concluded that what God hath cleansed they are not to call common. The prevailing feeling in this city today is one of thankfulness for the coming of a man, who by his winsome personality, his popular address, his loyalty to the truth, his personal piety, has made a lasting impression on a multitude of people and been the central figure in the greatest revival this city has ever experienced.

With more than **2,000** converted in **Fulton County** within a month, it is safe to say that her people will ever have a warm place in their hearts for W. E. Geil.

(The Daily Leader., February 25, 1895, Page 9)

ADDISON, NY

GEIL CLOSES SALOONS

Evangelist W. E. Geil, who successfully conducted revival meetings here last winter, is creating a stir in Addison, NY, according to a dispatch in the *New York Press*, which is as follows: "**There is great religious excitement in this region. The young evangelist, W. E. Geil of Doylestown, PA, closed tonight the most remarkable union Gospel meetings this place has ever witnessed. A big tent has been crowded nightly, and many have not been able to gain admittance.**

"All business places and saloons have been closed during the services. The most prominent men in the community have been interested in the movement, and hundreds have announced that they had been converted. Mr. Geil speaks in **Fort Plain, *NY*,** Thursday evening."
(The Daily Leader., October 02, 1895, Page 5)

HERKIMER, NY

Evangelist W. E. Geil closed a very successful series of meetings at **Herkimer** last week. **As a result of the meetings, 537 persons were converted; and the churches in Herkimer quickened into life. During the stay in Herkimer, Mr. Geil preached 21 sermons to audiences averaging 1,200 nightly**.
(The Daily Leader., January 10, 1895, Page 8, Image 8)

BROADALBIN, MAYFIELD, AND NORTHVILLE, NY

W. E. Geil who had such great success in conducting revival services at **Broadalbin, NY,** some time ago, has been at work in **Mayfield, NY,** where he secured **over 250 converts.** He will for the present be at **Northville, NY,** where he will hold meetings. We were told this morning that an effort was being made to secure the services of Mr. Geil and have him conduct meetings in this village *(Johnstown, NY).*

(The Johnstown Daily Republican., Volume, August 30, 1894, Page 7)

CHAPTER 8

WAVES OF REVIVAL WASH OVER OCEAN GROVE, NEW JERSEY

It's hard to believe that 50,000 people met back in 1894 for Camp Meeting in Ocean Grove, NJ. There were so many people in attendance that they had to meet at different locations throughout the city. It's interesting to note that there were pastors from every state in the Union.

To put this in perspective, on New Year's Eve, 2019, a crowd of approximately 64,000 people filled Mercedes-Benz Stadium in Atlanta, GA, to usher in the New Year with praise and worship. This was a huge gathering!

INTERESTING TO METHODISTS
And to Others Who Attend
the Ocean Grove Camp Meetings

The Ocean Grove Camp Meeting Association has begun the erection of a huge, new auditorium at that popular Methodist summer resort on the Jersey coast, and it is expected to be ready for use in time for the meetings of the coming summer. The new building is to be 224 feet in depth by 161 feet in width and will have a seating capacity of 9,500. The roof will be 85 feet high in the center, with a slope to the sides, where it will be 50 feet from the ground. There are to be four towers, of which the main one will be 125 feet in height. Nothing will be left undone that mechanical skill and ingenuity could suggest to make the building the most complete and best appointed structure of its kind in the world. One novelty in its construction will be the arrangement of the rear and side walls into three tiers of movable panels so that the auditorium may be either wholly or partially enclosed in inclement weather or thrown entirely open to the ocean breezes on the sultry summer days. The flooring will be of asphalt and will have an easy incline from the rear and sides toward the platform, affording an unbroken view of the rostrum and speakers. The acoustic properties have been carefully considered, and the architect, F. T. Camp, says that 90 percent of the largest audience will have no difficulty in hearing every word.

(Olean Herald., February 27, 1894, Page 2)

CAMP MEETING AT OCEAN GROVE

Ocean Grove Camp Meeting
Monday, August 20th

The Annual Camp Meeting of the
Ocean Grove Association Began

ASBURY PARK, NJ

Aug. 23—Fully **50,000 people** assembled at the various meetings of the annual camp meeting at Ocean Grove yesterday, **the largest gathering in its history**. Among the prominent clergymen officiating were Rev. S. M. Vernon of Lancaster, Pa., T. L. Paulson of Brooklyn, H. W. Lawrence of New York, D. B. Updegraff of Mr. Pleasant, O. W. L. S. Murray of Wilmington, Del., and G. W. Miller of Kansas City. **The clergy present represented every state in the Union.**

(The Chronicle., August 23, 1894, Page 5)

OCEAN GROVE CAMP MEETING

Today the Great Religious Gathering at Asbury Park Will Disperse

ASBURY PARK, NJ

Aug. 30—There is no abatement in the attendance at the great **Ocean Grove** Camp Meeting. Last night there was a big turnout to attend the last evening service of the camp. Rev. Thomas L. Poulson, of Jamaica, Long Island, addressed an audience of over **5,000**. Today is the closing day of the camp meeting.

The baptism of infants took place at 9 o'clock, and this will be followed by the administration of the Lord's Supper at 3 o'clock this afternoon.

(Daily Leader., August 30, 1894, Page 1)

SUNDAY PREACHES TO 7,500 AT ASBURY

Address Opens Fiftieth Jubilee Camp Meeting

ASBURY PARK, NJ

Aug. 23—The Rev. Billy Sunday preached his first sermon here this morning to about 7,500 people in the Ocean Grove Auditorium. The occasion is the fiftieth jubilee camp meeting being held here. Sunday will preach twice a day until a week from tomorrow.

In the sermon today, Sunday showed all of his old-time fire and picturesque activity. The subject was, "The Hour Has

Struck," and Sunday devoted much of his time to an arrangement of the present style of preaching.

"The day has passed," he said, "when preachers can continue to deliver deodorized sermons in tabloid form." The churches must realize, he asserted, that they are a means to an end and not an end themselves. He was especially hard on the conservative church, describing the old-fashioned deacon as an "old fossil who has taken so many pills that his joints are ball bearing."

(The Sun., August 24, 1919, Page 15, Image 15)

Dr. Brennan To Preach at Ocean Grove Meeting[1]

The Rev. Harold Roy Brennan, minister of St. Mark's Methodist Church, will preach at the Ocean Grove Camp Meeting from August 27 through September 1. Also preaching there will be **Billy Graham, famous evangelist,** and Leonard H. Cochran, a member of the General Board of Missions of the Methodist Church. The Ocean Grove Camp Meeting was founded by Methodist preachers and laymen in 1869. **The auditorium in Ocean Grove, NJ, has a seating capacity of 10,000 persons.** Dr. Brennan received the Freedom Foundation Award for three years and last year was selected as the National Exchange Preacher to Great Britain.

(The Long Island News and The Owl., Friday, August 26, 1955)

CHAPTER 9

REVIVAL AND AWAKENING

THE 100-YEAR PROPHECIES

There are several 100-year prophecies from near the year 1900, which state that God is going to pour out His Spirit in a more powerful way than ever before and that we will see worldwide revival and awakening. Both Maria Woodworth-Etter and William Seymour prophesied about this coming end-time revival that will sweep across the face of this earth. I believe that we are in the birthing stages of this final outpouring of God's Glory upon Earth.

Many of the revivals that you read about in this book can help to spur us on in our faith to believe God that right now, He wants to do something extraordinary on this planet.

Pastor Michael Edds wrote the following article, and he gave us permission to share it with you in this book.

Great Spiritual Awakenings have swept the world over the centuries. They have changed lives and the very culture in which we live. An Awakening is a special time when God comes down and saturates a place and a people with His presence. There is a final Great Awakening coming.

The Final Great Awakening–
An End-time Revival

*The great Azusa Street Awakening, which over the years
resulted in 600 million being swept into the Kingdom of God
and gave birth to the Pentecostal Movement, began in 1906. It
was one of the greatest outpourings of the Spirit of God since
Pentecost. Multitudes were saved, healed, and filled with the
Holy Spirit. Incredible miracles occurred.*

*This great revival moved from Los Angeles to its new
focal point of Chicago, Illinois. The two great centers of revival
in Chicago were the North Avenue Mission and the Stone
Church. Pentecost swept from Chicago to Canada, Europe,
South America, and Africa. One of the greatest outpourings
occurred at Stone Church in 1913. The renowned evangelist
Maria Woodworth-Etter began a revival on July 2, 1913 at
Stone Church.*

*The services were to last until the end of July but
continued for six months. This was a time of divine appointment
for the city of Chicago; God rent the heavens and came down!
Scenes from the days of the Early Church began to occur at
Stone Church. Word began to spread throughout Chicago of
miraculous healings, deliverance from demonic possession,
conversions, and of the outpouring of the Holy Spirit happening
in these meetings. Advertisement was no longer necessary! The
city was incredibly shaken.*

*Word spread of the miraculous intervention of God.
Thousands came on trolleys, buggies, and trains, while many
walked. Some came from distances of 1,600 miles away. 1,200
to 1,500 packed into Stone Church each night. The basement
was filled, and many stood out on the street. Street meetings
were held to accommodate them. Three services were held on
Sundays!*

As Christians prayed around the altar one evening, Sister Woodworth-Etter and others gave the following powerful prophecy and divine promise, which they prophesied would occur within 100 years of the 1913 Chicago Visitation. She prophesied of this coming End Time Revival....

"We are not yet up to the fullness of the Former Rain and that when the Latter Rain comes, it will far exceed anything we have seen!"

Rev. William Seymour, the leader of the Azusa Street Awakening, also prophesied that **in 100 years there would be an outpouring of God's Spirit and His Shekinah Glory that would be greater and more far reaching than what was experienced at Azusa.**

It has been almost 100 years since these prophecies were given. In my own beloved church, I am seeing the beginnings of this prophecy being fulfilled.... Healing and miracles are occurring! The anointing of the Holy Spirit on the services is heavy and growing each week. Something IS happening! I believe that we have reached the time of the fulfillment of these 100-year-old prophecies. We must be diligent to pray, intercede, and protect what the Lord is doing. We must encourage and edify one another as never before. We must crucify every critical, judgmental, and religious spirit that may be within us. We must put on the holiness and righteousness of Christ. Our time of divine destiny has come. We are about to experience what Brother Seymour and Sister Woodworth-Etter foresaw. God is about to rend the heavens and come down! The greatest revival in the history of the church is at hand!

Be encouraged, God is on the Move in our generation!

CHAPTER 10

THREE KEYS TO USHERING IN REVIVAL AND AWAKENING

Over the years, I have come to understand that there are three keys that are crucial to positioning ourselves to receive from and to be used by God. These three are all important, kind of like the legs of a birthing stool. If one is absent, the whole stool will be off balance. If we want to usher in revival and awakening and allow God to birth through us what He desires right now, then we need to be mindful of these three keys.

1. Walking in UNITY in the LOVE of GOD

There is no "I" in "TEAM," and there are no lone rangers in the Body of Christ.

I have a dream of a day when Christians will no longer be defined by their denomination or where they attend church, but they will be defined by whether or not they are a child of God. It will be a wonderful day when denominational barriers are torn down, and many people who love Jesus will come together for special services and events to worship and praise Him and pray together as one Body.

In John 17:20-23, we read the prayer that Jesus prayed for all believers everywhere, including each one of us: *"I do not*

pray for these alone, but also for those who will believe in Me
through their word; that they all may be one, as You, Father,
are in Me, and I in You; that they also may be one in Us, that
the world may believe that You sent Me. And the glory which
You gave Me I have given them, that they may be one just as
We are one: I in them, and You in Me; that they may be made
perfect in one, and that the world may know that You have
sent Me, and have loved them as You have loved Me."

It always amazes me when I think about this portion of scripture—to think that 2,000 years ago, Jesus prayed for you and me to walk in unity with Him and with other believers. He could have prayed about so many other things, but this must be very important since it is one of the things that He focused on.

Why is UNITY so important that Jesus prayed it for each one of us? Because it reveals how the world will be drawn to Jesus.... By watching how we who are Christians walk in love—they'll know we are Christians **by our love for one another** (John 13:35).

We have to let go of the denominational and doctrinal differences that separate us and walk in unity as Jesus prayed for us to do. If a belief won't keep us out of Heaven, then it shouldn't separate us from working together for the Kingdom of God while we're here on the planet. We need to respect one another and recognize that differences in Bible interpretation that are not salvation issues should not separate us.

This doesn't mean that we're advocating for a one-world religion or that we agree with everything that another brother or sister in Christ believes, but that we recognize that people who put their trust in Jesus as Lord and Savior of their lives are part of the family of God. Every one of us will be surprised when we get to Heaven and see just how many things that we have believed to be absolutes that weren't quite the way that we thought they were.

God may have people connected in different denominations because He has different calls on both their lives and their churches. If we can recognize this, then we won't feel the need to convince others to become more like us. Our hearts' desire should be that they become more like Jesus and walk in their own call.

Just because someone doesn't worship with the same style of music or have the same style of delivery of the Word that we do, doesn't mean that they are not right with God.

In Mark 9:38-41, it says: *Now John answered Him, saying, "Teacher, we saw someone who does not follow us casting out demons in Your name, and we forbade him because he does not follow us."* (NKJV)

*But Jesus said, "Do not forbid him, for no one who works a miracle in My name can soon afterward speak evil of Me. **For he who is not against us is on our side.** For whoever gives you a cup of water to drink in My name, because you belong to Christ, assuredly, I say to you, he will by no means lose his reward."*

You might say, "But the Bible says, 'Study to shew thyself approved unto God, a workman that needeth not to be ashamed, rightly dividing the word of truth'" (2 Timothy 2:15, KJV). And yes, it does say that. But for many years, we have taken this God-breathed scripture, which is meant to encourage us to know why we believe what we believe, and used it as an excuse for spiritual pride and division. Oh, how this must grieve the heart of God!

He delights when His people dwell together in UNITY.

Psalm 133:1-3 (NKJV)
Behold, how good and how pleasant it is
For brethren to dwell together in unity!
It is like the precious oil upon the head,
Running down on the beard,
The beard of Aaron,
Running down on the edge of his garments.
It is like the dew of Hermon,
Descending upon the mountains of Zion;
For there the LORD commanded the blessing—
Life forevermore.

If we want to be in the place where God commands His life-giving blessing, then we need to walk in unity with our true sisters and brothers in Christ.

2. PRAYER (Personal and Corporate)

*"if **My people** who are **called by My name** will **humble themselves**, and **pray** and **seek My face**, and **turn from their wicked ways**, then **I will hear from heaven**, and will **forgive their sin** and **heal their land**."* 2 Chronicles 7:14 (NKJV)

God is looking for a people who will humbly go before Him in **repentance and with faith-filled prayers, believing that He will do what He said He will do.** If we truly want to hear from Heaven, then it is important for us to pray both individually as well as corporately. There has never been a REVIVAL that has not been preceded by prayer.

1 John 1:9 says: **"If we confess our sins, He is faithful and just to forgive us our sins** and to cleanse us from all unrighteousness." We need to confess our sins and turn from them so that nothing will hinder our prayers, and we will be more fully usable by God. We also need to forgive ourselves

and move on, because we have work to do for the Kingdom of God.

Learn to listen to the voice of God in prayer. A revival will come as you follow the leading of the Holy Spirit. Don't just jump out and do something because it's a good idea. Hear from the Father what His will is in Heaven right now, and pray like Jesus did—that Heaven will come to Earth. What is the Father showing you to do right now? Get God's heart through prayer, and be led by the Holy Spirit.

My heart's cry is: "Revive us again, O Lord!"

3. OBEDIENCE (Walking in Holiness)

"If you love Me, keep My commandments." John 14:1 (NKJV)

Obedience is not merely a suggestion; it was commanded by Jesus Himself. Let's ask God to work in each of our hearts, to help us to be more like Jesus each day, and to send us forth into the world to share with people just how much God loves them.

My prayer for each of you is that God will fuel the spark that's already in your heart into a full flame, that you will be set on fire for Jesus, be full of the Holy Spirit and power, and be a bright light to the lost in this world in these last days. If you are already on fire for Jesus, **I pray that you will burn even more brightly**.

Jesus was our example, and this is how He walked:
*Let this mind be in you, which was also in **Christ Jesus**: Who, being in the form of God, thought it not robbery to be equal with God: **But made himself of no reputation, and took upon him the form of a servant, and was made in the likeness of men**: And being found in fashion as a man, he humbled himself, and became obedient unto death, even the death of the cross.*

Wherefore God also hath highly exalted him, and given him a name which is above every name: That at the name of Jesus every knee should bow, of things in heaven, and things in earth, and things under the earth; And that every tongue should confess that Jesus Christ is LORD, to the glory of God the Father. Philippians 2:5-11 (KJV)

We have to be careful not to try to make a reputation for ourselves and to always point people to God.

He who says he abides in Him (Jesus) *ought himself also to walk just as He walked.* 1 John 2:6 (NKJV)

As our friend, Dean Braxton, says, "Everything that God created acts in the manner that it was created to. A tree acts like a tree; a fish acts like a fish; and a Christian ought to act like a Christian! Act like who you are!"

IN CLOSING

I pray that this book has been thought provoking and challenging for you and that it will raise your level of faith and expectation regarding full-blown revival and awakening in this present hour that we're living in. Let's be open to allowing God to move—His way, in our day! There are many other things that I could have shared, but I believe that these are the things that **God wants me to focus on right now … FOR SUCH A TIME AS THIS.**

May God bless you, prepare you, strengthen you, lead you, guide you, give you wisdom, and use you to help bring in the final harvest of souls in these last days in which we're living. This is an exciting time to be alive!

SALVATION PRAYER

If you don't already know Jesus as your Lord and Savior and you want to, please pray the following prayer from deep within your heart to enter into a relationship with Him:

Dear Jesus,
I admit that I'm a sinner, and I need You. Thank you for dying on the cross in my place and taking my punishment. Please forgive me for my sins and come into my heart and be my Savior and my Lord. Please help me to live for You from this day forward. Thank you for making me part of Your family. In Jesus' Name, Amen.

If you prayed this prayer sincerely from your heart, you are now a child of God. You have just taken your first step in your journey with Him. Welcome to His family!

INDEX

Broadalbin – 66
Brooklyn – 5, 7
Buffalo – 7
Cambridge – 25
Center White Creek – 25
Clyde – 31
Cobleskill – 34
Cohoes – 3, 8
Crown Point – 42, 43
Gloversville – 54, 62
Granville – 55
Greenwich – 24, 25, 26
Ellenburgh Depot – 52
Fort Plain – 65
Glens Falls – 53
Hague – 42
Herkimer – 65
Howes Cave – 33
Hudson – 3
Hudson (Along River) – 17
Hudson Falls – 3
   (Sandy Hill)
Johnstown – 54, 66
Lansingburgh – 3
Mamaroneck – 17
Mayfield – 66
Northville – 66
New York City – 4, 8, 12, 13
Potsdam – 58
Poughkeepsie – 61
Saratoga – 8, 10, 59
Schenectady – 7, 9, 34
Ticonderoga – 35, 36, 37, 38, 39, 41, 42
Troy – 2, 3
Truthville – 59

Utica – 6
Waterford – 3, 8
West Troy – 3, 10
White Creek – 3, 26
Whitehall – 61

NORTH CAROLINA – 27

OHIO
Cincinnati – 6
Circleville – 15
Cleveland – 7, 28
Clinton County – 27
Scioto – 27

PENNSYLVANIA
Philadelphia – 6, 12, 17, 38, 60
Scranton – 28

ROHDE ISLAND
Pawtucket – 9
Providence – 6, 9

SOUTH CAROLINA
Charleston – 2

TENNESSEE
Memphis – 2, 57

VERMONT
Burlington – 14, 52
Western Border Towns – 13

VIRGINIA
Parkersburg – 28
Pittsburgh – 10
Richmond – 21
Taylor County – 12

WEST VIRGINIA
Huntington – 28
Mt. Elkhorn – 28

AUSTRALIA
Tasmania – 49

CANADA – 1, 59, 60, 72
Toronto – 60

CHINA – 49

ENGLAND – 43, 53
London – 20, 21

INDIA – 22, 23

IRELAND – 49

JAPAN – 49

SCOTLAND – 49

WALES – 23, 48, 49

ACKNOWLEDGMENTS

A MIGHTY MAN OF GOD

Reverend Jim Peterson

Pastor Jim Peterson went home to be with the Lord on Friday, January 31, 2020. He had the heart of a revivalist and served the Lord faithfully for over 50 years—always trying to bring the people of God together in unity in every community that he ministered in. He labored in the field, tilling up the fallow ground. We are blessed that now we are about to reap the harvest for which he had labored for so long. I will be forever grateful for his example and encouragement in my life.

A DEAR FRIEND AND BROTHER IN CHRIST

Reverend Dean Braxton

I thank God for this Godly man who is also a mentor and a friend. His encouragement, guidance, and insight from Heaven has changed my life completely; and it is partially because of his advice that this book is being published. Because of Dean's impact on my life, I will never be the same.

PHOTOGRAPHER

Robbie Batchelor

Thank you for generously providing the photo for the back cover of this book.

BIBLIOGRAPHY

Chapter 2: REVIVAL TRIVIA

1. The Greenwich Journal and Salem Press, Used with written permission on February 11, 2020.

Chapter 3: HUGE REVIVAL AT HOWES CAVE—1880

1. https://www.tripsavvy.com/howe-caverns-photo-tour-ny-caves-1601034, Used with permission, January 13, 2020.

Chapter 8: WAVES OF REVIVAL CRASH OVER OCEAN GROVE, NEW JERSEY

1. Herald Community Newspapers and Communications, Inc., Copyright © 1955 Richner Communications, Inc., Used with written permission and contract on January 18, 2020.

Chapter 9: REVIVAL AND AWAKENING – THE 100-YEAR PROPHECIES

1. https://greatawakening.blogspot.com/, Used with permission, January 2020.

Made in the USA
Middletown, DE
10 May 2022

65569724R00060